STATE OF A SUNFLOWER SOUL

State of a Sunflower Soul

by Dabria Karapita-Parker

State of a Sunflower Soul
Copyright © 2024 by Dabria Karapita-Parker.

All rights reserved. This book or any portion thereof may not be reproduced or used in any manner whatsoever without the express written permission of the author except for the use of brief quotations in the context of reviews.

ISBN: 978-1-7383879-0-8

Book design & layout by Rachel Clift.
rcliftpoetry.com

First printing edition, 2024.

dkpcreatives.com
Dabria Karapita-Parker

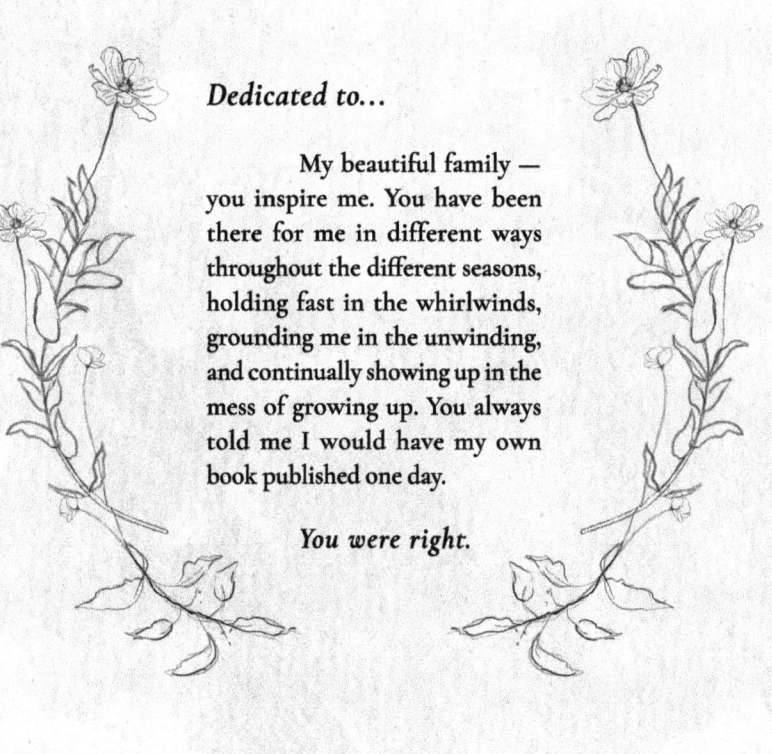

Dedicated to...

My beautiful family —
you inspire me. You have been
there for me in different ways
throughout the different seasons,
holding fast in the whirlwinds,
grounding me in the unwinding,
and continually showing up in the
mess of growing up. You always
told me I would have my own
book published one day.

You were right.

Contents

I. The End 1

II. Graveyard Shift 27

III. Nightfall. 59

IV. The Unwinding 79

V. Storyteller 109

VI. Polaroid Memories 135

VII. Sunlit Possibilities 159

VIII. (Aftermath) 187

IX. Summer/Autumn 215

X. Prologue 239

BE AWARE:
I'm a writer. Anything you do or say might end up in a book someday.
This book is a work of art, crafted from the inkwells of my heart. And you know what they say... life imitates art, and truth is often stranger than fiction.

I'm *probably* not writing about you.
Or you.

Poems

The End

*this is a story just like any other
with a beginning, middle, and end
and like most stories
it doesn't arrive at any of them
in the way we've come to expect*

02 • 14 • 19
the temperature is dropping
and we reminisce
about times gone by
the memories we've made

you just came inside from boosting my car
your nose is cold
our feet are entwined
and we bounce back and forth
on the experiences we've shared

we've had a lot of good times
and definitely some bad
that is simply the state of life
we carve a life out of the journey
and we never stop growing

when the cold is here, my love
remind me of sunflowers
their heads turning to the light
remind me of starlight
and the dreams we've painted
on the canvas of our future

remind me of mountains
all the heights we've faced
their beauty, their edges
their outline against the sky

remind me of us

Day 257
he says that he loves me
the sad thing is,
i think he loves himself more

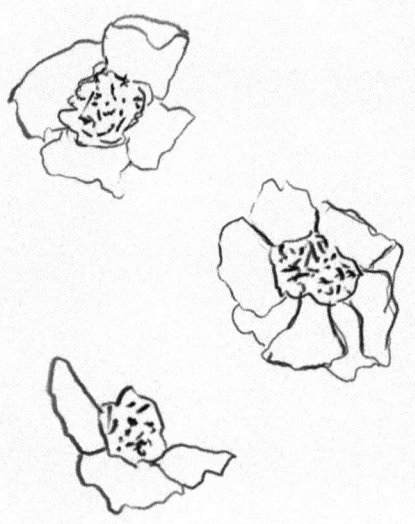

Dabria Karapita-Parker

i don't know how to reconcile the man i married
with the man you've become

-soul questions

it's odd
how **sex** permeates everything
the action of doing
or the depriving of

both can morph into a bottomless well

Dabria Karapita-Parker

who would've thought
that two becoming one
would leave me feeling more lonely in the end
than if i were truly alone

double standards
a mirrored reality
we are who we say we are
until we're more of what we do
we wait for the other shoe to drop

or we force the hand until it does

Dabria Karapita-Parker

i keep myself busy
like a top spinning, spinning
the faster i twirl
the less time i have to focus
on the sadness that threatens
to come searing through

State of a Sunflower Soul

i only get drunk when i'm with you,
he says
and i wonder
if that's whispered regret
that lingers in his voice

Dabria Karapita-Parker

he shifts away in the dark
and i am left falling asleep
in the cave of a dark room
utterly on my own
what happened to our midnight caresses?
when did i become a silent body, an unsmiling face
in a room full of white noise?
when did we stop falling
(**in love**)
and i start falling
(**alone**)?

State of a Sunflower Soul

i don't think you know, i don't think you realize,
i don't think you care
you became an immovable boulder
set in the wet cement where you had fallen
i was only resting, waiting to rise
on eagle's wings to the next level
you couldn't handle the potential drop
that soaring in the heights brings
so instead,

you just tried to drag me back down

i want to reach for you
you are the limb on the tree
i thought we were nurturing to grow
turns out you were waiting to make it into a show

the axe taken to the bark swinging
a swirling pattern of leaves falling

Fighting Thoughts
that moment when all the fairy tales look grim
because you finally realize what they *didn't* say
this is no happily ever after
this is the moment right after you realize:

you are in this alone

Dabria Karapita-Parker

i am deeply wounded
i look in the mirror and see the black stains
running down my cheeks
i notice the balloons of disbelief beneath my eyes
i am a dust particle
wiped away with a single lie
i am a floater
someone who has been booted from her own mind
the projection of belief which i had hung from the draperies
lie closed and darkened because of a sentence said
a decision made
a telltale sign misread

False Family
it was foolish of me to feel
that i could come to lay at the same spot
where others hold your heart
i am but a well-loved intruder
cared for, watched over
but never in the same degree
when push comes to shove
your loyalties lie
in the beauties that were melded from your heart
how can I blame you?
i am but a well-loved intruder

Dabria Karapita-Parker

i feel sad
that my body has became a chore to you
instead of
finding delight in one another,
it is a leakage of boredom
that runs out from your veins

Soft Heart, Healed Scars
my dad raised a tough girl
i don't bruise, i bleed
and when i heal, i scar
they want to hide truth?
let them break bones

i've healed them before.

Dabria Karapita-Parker

why are people
always searching
for something
that will numb them?

feeling everything is better than feeling nothing at all

he has opened up caverns inside me
broken apart the formed walls of my childhood
i am no longer the girl of afore
i am someone new, unearthed
and not yet complete
what is this new vision of myself i see?

Dabria Karapita-Parker

i cry in the shadows
momma raised a bleeder
not a whiner
i wipe the crimson from my knees
and the rivers from my cheeks
i may cry in the shadows
but i rise from the meadows
of the woods and roots i was raised from
and the trees of strength i've forged for myself

State of a Sunflower Soul

i look up at the lilac sky
my breath dancing in the icy air
i thought we matched
yet perhaps there were unseen cracks
hidden in the seams
i wouldn't go so far as to call us mismatched puzzle pieces
forced into place
(there was no force. you made free choice.)
it was you and i
choosing forever, together
we were the ones supposed to decide which way to go
(you alone chose to veer off that path)

Dabria Karapita-Parker

i don't know how to live
with these unfulfilled longings
and aching questions
so i stare at pretty sunsets
letting the music wash over my skin
flow through my veins
releasing the need to have all the
answers
finally allowing myself to simply be

State of a Sunflower Soul

i used to listen
to the reverberations
of the heartbeat
in your chest
until one day,
there was a strong wall
where there used to be a heart

Graveyard Shift

October 20, 2018
kisses soon to be in a graveyard
under a blanket of stars
the canopy of trees
envelope us in their web of arms
it's almost spooky season,
they whisper to us
just give it two years and nine months and four days
and you wait, it'll be quite the scare

sometimes hindsight is a graveyard we hold in our hearts.

Tunnel Vision
and that night
the stars were maddeningly bright
in a sky of midnight blue
i thought to myself
(deep down)
i think I really like you

08/10/2018

when they asked me
how i felt about him
i simply replied,

"butterflies"

i think what scared me the most about you
was that i could look at you
and almost glimpse my future

(you are in it. a door is swinging)

Dabria Karapita-Parker

it was a gentle wind that swept you in
you were comfort in a red flannel
it was your quiet confidence that made
me want to dance in your breeze

and it was (terrifying)
that you wanted me so

and it was (incredible)
that you wanted me so

it was also the most painful blow to my heart
to find out you had travelled these corridors before
what if i become just another one of "those girls" to you?

i don't want to be another wax figure
in the museum of your heart

11/10/2018

11pm Prayers
that was the night i decided
i could no longer be afraid
of the scribbled past
i could no longer be afraid
of what the unknown future may hold

these are my prayers.
for you.
for me.
for us.

i relinquish them to God.

08/10/2018

you asked me what i had to hope for
and i whispered back softly,
"you."

i try to describe this slow
awakening
this unfurling of petals,
of desire

Leap of Faith
i stood on the face of the cliff
staring down into the abyss of possibility
trusting you to hold my heart
to never lie
to remind me that i can fly
fingers spread wide
to feel the wind
i looked up into the sky
i closed my eyes
then i
                      jumped

12/10/2018

Dabria Karapita-Parker

someone once gave me this tender advice
telling me that once i knew i was safe
i should allow myself to gloriously fall

this is me free falling

19/10/2018

Give me all of you.
i've always loved the ocean
with its rippling currents
deep beauty
and colourful mystery
i desire to swim in its deepest depths

can't you see? this is a metaphor.

i have this vague awareness of you
(we are sitting in the car, pointing at the stars
my fingers curled inside of your palms)
and i ask myself if this is real
if what i'd always imagined
could possibly be sitting in the leather seat next to me
if this goodness could simply have sprung from
something so unexpected
as you walking through the door
of a place you'd never been before

29/10/2018

i keep praying that there will never come a day
when you look at me with eyes that don't say,
you're what i've been waiting for
i can't believe you're mine
i'll fight for you
with my life

Dabria Karapita-Parker

suddenly i didn't care
that there had been other girls before
i just wanted to be the one and only
you desired to hold

30/10/2018

we're sitting in your parked car
my head leaning against your chest
our breaths intermingle in the chilly air
as i smile with contentment
i wonder to myself
is this peace?
and
is it truly mine?

02/11/2018

Dabria Karapita-Parker

i hope i *never* have reason to stop writing poetry about you...

14/11/2018

you let me be myself
you honoured that within me

that is one of the most beautiful gifts anyone has given me

20/11/2018

Hopeful Future

you reached for me and wiped my tears
you held me close and quieted my fears
you gently stroked my hand
(palm on palm, a soothing balm)

my friend described you as having a steady character
a strong heart
as i've gotten to know you deeply
i couldn't agree more

25/11/2018

State of a Sunflower Soul

he says i'm the moon
with all of her phases
while i know he's the sun
with the comfort of
a steady warmth

Dabria Karapita-Parker

i told you i could look at us and see forever
to which you replied,
>*"for always."*

Birthday Gift
i am swaying in a red dress
slow dancing
your hand pressed against mine
foreheads touching
music in both our hearts
(no one hears it but us)

i am certain. this is perfection.

22/12/2018

Growing
when i met you
the connection which grew
made all the others i'd made
feel like simple child's play

gratitude for the practice grows stems
in the flowerbed of my heart

State of a Sunflower Soul

we draw constellations on each other's noses
touch the other's leg with our toes
dreaming of the future as we look into each other's eyes

they used to tell me i dream too big
now all i can think is
they were all so very wrong
because you exceed my wildest dreams

i love the way you sing in the shower

i'm walking down a hallway
a single light shines at its end
it's a future with you i see.

i love the way you make me want to sing in the shower

late night coffee shops
a skyline of city lights
walking arm and arm into our future
on the snow-dusted winter streets.

somewhere in the future i turn the shower on

Needlework
sometimes
you meet a person
and they become so engrained
into the very fabric of your life
all of your hopes and imaginings
rest between the blades of their shoulders
you're no longer afraid
of having to one day rip them out
you know they're sewn in to stay

16/01/2019

moonlight
starlight
we stay up talking half the night
sunrise
snowfall
gentle footsteps down the hall
daybreak
clouds dissipate
you and i
stay in each other's arms
and love each other half-awake
midday
sun peaks
you say you'll stay
forever with me
real life begins to form from the dream
afternoon turns into evening
and we begin it all over again

The Dream
then it happened
one day
i started dreaming again
and i almost started to cry
because there i was
looking into your blue eyes
i would see myself reflected
a few years in the future
leaning down on the ground
with our dog (or two)
welcoming you back from work
in the porch of our very own home
suddenly it's all so clear
i smile at the man sitting here
thinking to myself,
you truly are my future now

Nightfall

Two years later...

Dabria Karapita-Parker

i am driven to distraction by the knotted mess
you have made with my heart roots
what a grave mistake it was that night
we flung our hearts out among the stars
walking through a graveyard of all the mistakes of lovers past
little did we know our hearts were soon to join their corpses
(you dug their separate grave, day by married day)

Ring on wedding ring
you treated your acceptance of me as a gift to bestow
instead of taking pleasure in my hand you got to hold
while i was happy just to exist in the throne room of your heart
you felt deserving to be king alone from the start
and threw me off our jointed throne

they say love makes you do crazy things
climb mountains, breathe fire, spread wings
what love does **not** do
is instill fear into the heart of the woman

you once vowed till death do you part

State of a Sunflower Soul

you scare me
with your ability to weave
such finely threaded silver lies
sparkling, shining
intricately ornate
covering a throne of tall tales

i am everyone's best friend
and yet no one is mine
the kitchen floor holds me in its embrace
and the walls have heard me shouting through pain
loneliness is an aching limb
and a crack
and a bruise deep within
from all the times i have kept my mouth shut
and all the times you have poured out your weighty words
onto my heavy shoulders
i have gotten so good at being your friend
it's only on the tough nights i wish someone was mine

State of a Sunflower Soul

i think you broke my heart
in a million tiny ways
and then you broke my trust
all at once

what do i do with this finality?

Dabria Karapita-Parker

Compete
i love you
anger coming on an escalator
i love you more
locks changed on our front door
i love you most
give me what i want or i'll take you to court

but you see, in the end, i loved me and you the most
because i was the first to let the anger go

one moment you're saying, "*i do*"
and the next,
all your actions are
i don't, i don't, i don't
what is this strange version of love?
where one minute you're vowing forever
and the next,
bowing out?

Dabria Karapita-Parker

you promised me forever
then locked me out the door
when forever got too hard
and good-bye seemed
the easy route out

**my knuckles are bruised
from trying to claw my way in**

lies fall off peoples' lips so easily
the ones we keep, the ones we eat, the ones we stow
i should've known you would never show
(them)
it's all a game
but i always held out hope
(perhaps that was just another lie i told myself)

night creeps in and the darkness hovers
and i have no one to cling to

Red Light, Green Light

how is it that this one act of cliche methodology
becomes a staple in our lives
we brush our teeth as a notice to start the day
start
we brush our teeth as a way to finish the day
finish
you used to say "i love you"
as our way to start
now i whisper "no you don't"
as our way to end

it is interesting
how easy
someone can make it
for you to carve them
out of your life
and not want them to come back in

Dabria Karapita-Parker

you once told me that only dead fish go with the flow
you said you wanted the anger, the passion, the burn
and our make-ups were the salve that healed our wounds
but there came a point
when your desires switched
and it was no longer the thrashing, moving, breathing,
shiny fish you wanted
rather, one that has let go of life

how did we go from bathing in the river of life
to throwing it all away?

it's funny how
in the beginning
you were the one who created my prison
and it's funny how
in the end of it all
you were the one who gave me the key

or did i have to wrest it from your hands?

Dabria Karapita-Parker

today,
i said goodbye
to the job, the ring
the life i'd imagined

today,
i make space
for the next
whatever that may be

there is so much loss
it comes in waves
it's overwhelming
it threatens to drown me
in its bitter embrace

this is me reclaiming my power
this is me taking it all back
the things that haven't been coloured by him
this is the unwinding

The Unwinding

Dabria Karapita-Parker

i want to write my story
gently, torturously, honestly
doing justice to the time we spent together
while not destroying this time we are now set apart

Cycles
it used to be you who read my poetry
now it is you i write poetry about
the circle goes around
around
around
and is once again
complete

Dabria Karapita-Parker

you swung at me with a hammer
with the intention to wreck me
little did you know
this girl is made of steel

fire and heat are what make me

State of a Sunflower Soul

i feel nothing
nothing
except for relief

it is a bittersweet rock
a weight of pressure deep within

because,
if i met you on the street
i would turn to walk the other way

sometimes,
i am suspended in disbelief

sometimes,
i am content with the separate lives we now lead

sometimes,
i am drowning in a sea of rage

sometimes,
i am caught smiling at our memories

most times,
i am certain i will be alright

storms have always come and they will always pass
and rainbows are such a beautiful thing

i have an indent on my left hand
from where that metal wedding ring used to hang
and it is a cruel thing
the way your name keeps hanging off my tongue
why do i act like a hungry wolf
looking to devour a morsel of knowledge of you?
i bite it off and spit out blood
i swipe apologies from my lips
for all the many ways you echoed i failed
failed, failing, failure, fail
i wipe away the lying voices
i lay out on the ground in the middle of the ashes
"where do we go from here?"
whispers in the pumping of blood through veins

Life
it's okay to cry, darling girl
it's been one hell of a year
you've loved deeply
and lost much
yet there is still
so much life to live
much new love to give
there is more art to create
and when these feelings overwhelm
take a moment to breathe it in
and to allow yourself to feel it
don't numb it
there is so much more
it all waits on the other side of surrender

it's almost midnight
there is a gentle rain
the window by my bed captures its falling tears
it sounds like such a cliche but the coyotes are howling
and i'm unafraid
it's been 8 months and 21 days
since i felt safe
you remember that day?
it seemed such a little thing but that was when i knew
i was no longer safe
to be myself with you
who would know that this is where we would end up
two different sides of the same town
my relief washing my soul like rain

Dabria Karapita-Parker

i don't know
how to rip
you from my life
(in whispers and sighs and late night cries)

i don't know
how to come to terms
with the knowledge
that i am now alright
having torn you from my life
(in sunsets and poems and a lifetime of beautiful noise)

State of a Sunflower Soul

i don't listen to sad songs
because i'm not sad anymore
i remember lying next to you in bed
choking back the dam of tears
i remember lonely nights
a sahara desert between the sheets
i was crying out for love
and being told that what i had been given was good enough
i remember slowly starving
aching stomach
barely breathing

i don't listen to sad songs anymore
i listen to this resounding sound of freedom

Dabria Karapita-Parker

i don't think you understand
the fact that i don't miss you
it's not a phrase i'm just throwing out there
more and more i find that time is passing
without you occupying a millisecond of thought
and i am relieved
and i am angry
because for so long i felt bound by you
now that i am free i don't want to waste a moment
thinking of all that's been said and done

and so, i move on
(can i do that? just close this door?)

State of a Sunflower Soul

i pause
unwind
my tightened fingers from the clenches of my palms
loosen my shoulders
release the vibrant fear
there is no longer room for that here

slowly i begin to feel the exhaustion settle in
it's a bone deep feeling
i've been here before, i know how it goes
life has a funny way of bringing things back around
you never thought you'd need the same way again
breakup songs, old friends
long nights, healing thoughts

and so here i go
the surrender begins

sometimes i can still feel the shadow of you
trying to pull me back
to the headspace we had together
i won't go there
not again
you've wasted too much of my time
in that place of self-pity
i won't be a reflection of your choices
any longer

i look in the mirror and the girl with the big eyes refuses
to look back into the darkness of your mind

you always acted like it was such a
damned inconvenience to love me
as time went by
all i did was slowly shrink
the ways i asked you to do so
i made my dreams with you smaller
went from,
"i solemnly swear to love you through it all"
to,
"can you at least look at me and pretend you still love me?"

today, i make this vow to myself
i will shrink myself no more
i will not mark myself as a sinking hole
i will accept the love for myself you could never give me
and i will be at peace in this

State of a Sunflower Soul

i don't miss you
instead,
anxiety creeps into the crevices left
by all the ways you couldn't love me
if i saw you today
i wouldn't rush to you
you admired my flame and then exploded like dynamite
when i got too close
you say that's on me but who are we kidding
i always walked around with a bonfire in my chest
you were the one who enjoyed its warmth and then
decided you wanted the cold instead
so when i say goodbye know that this is the end
my spark can't be smothered anymore

Dabria Karapita-Parker

i think the biggest thing
i can now thank you for
is the fact that i'm feeling again
after being numb for so long

sometimes i feel a little bit cruel
for not missing you more
then i remember all of the not okay things you said and did
(to me, my family, my world, my life, my heart)
using the label of love tacked on hastily
as an afterthought
and all the many ways
my defences were not allowed to stand
my tears, my fears, my dreams
none of it was safe
from your mocking embrace

**I no longer think it is cruel to feel released
from the burden I became to you.**

Dabria Karapita-Parker

the leaves are changing colours
one season ends and another awakens from sleep
i feel like i've been here before
the end of the old
the beginning of the new

i'm never coming back
you listen to such sad songs, darling
almost as if you're surprised
that i don't have any desire to come back
to our rose garden with its roots lying dead

Dabria Karapita-Parker

there used to exist a well of love for you
inside of me
it has dried up now
day by day
i toss a spadeful of dirt inside of it
until one day
there will be fresh green
formed
from the forgotten draughts of the well

State of a Sunflower Soul

you dumped me
as easily as a child
throwing away an unwanted toy

i got over you
as easily as unlocking the door
to a house i've never been in before

so many new places to explore

Dabria Karapita-Parker

i close my eyes
with a sigh
waiting for the thoughts to invade
(they will come they will go they will fade)

State of a Sunflower Soul

i drag myself through the soil
my fingernails caked in the mud of my transformation
growing takes time
it is messy
this colliding
forming and curating this life from within
shedding the dead vine
(unwinding)
that which is no longer mine

i am
unhindered
by your ability to let me go so easily
for what sparrow cries when it is released
from its gilded, glinting cage?
let me tell you this:

it doesn't, it sings

I'm so lonely
so i plunge my hand into the ice cold waters of my loneliness
let the world stand alone
i go back to all of our spots
reclaim them one by one
this one's still mine
now this one
this one
this one
i do not miss you
i miss our memories
and i will live in them once again
tell my stories
then kill them, softly
like laying my head on the cuttings of fresh grass
fragrant as they die

Storyteller

Dabria Karapita-Parker

i try to soften my words
wipe the malice from my fingertips
lick the anger off my lips
we poets have always bled ink and passion
write it down, let it go
i refuse to let the words make me something i am not

-vengeful

Pumpkin Walk

i remember when you wanted me to meet your mom and dad
and you told me later they were afraid i would be offended
by the silly things they sometimes say
i wish i could go back and touch their hands,
whisper they don't know me yet
the hard truth doesn't scare me, with its steely, unflinching gaze
the biggest spook i would tell that girl of nineteen to watch for
would be the jack o'lantern of your hidden intentions

this is a Halloween tale, after all

Dabria Karapita-Parker

i've missed old friends more than i've missed you
this sadness that permeates
it isn't for you
it's for me
for the life i'd imagined
for the loss i've been dealt
for the dreams i had held on to
and have had to release

it's no secret that you were the ripped page from our story
the anger, the distance, the finality
it's no mystery
you lost control and you did what cannot be undone
you slapped away the olive branch i held out to you

i will not hold myself as martyr for the actions
you chose to make alone

you made me promise never to smoke a cigarette again
rage leaking from the pores of your skin
seventeen days after i left
i released myself from the promise
made to a man
who hadn't kept his vow
as the cage around me cracked open
i took a long drag of freedom

**one moment you wake up and realize
that you will no longer be stifled**

you were simply too young,
i can hear your mother saying to you
patting your head and handing you your favourite, Irish stew

i remember when i was your favourite
we were in battle as partners
we were going to defy the odds
in it together, forever
i remember when that mantra was my favourite

somewhere, you take another bite of stew.

mama bear turned out to be a werewolf
sharpening her claws behind my back
don't you dare hurt my baby boy
she snarled
smiling on the other side of the altar
knowing, in the end
she'd get him back

Goldfish Memory
dear ex best friend
yes, it's me
the girl you once told everything to
dear ex best friend
yes, it's me
the girl you gave her first kiss to
dear ex best friend
yes, it's me
the passenger you drove across the country with
the one you were stuck in quarantine with
the woman you bought our first house with
the promise you stood on an altar with
dear ex best friend
do you remember it's me?
i don't think you do
because if you had
you wouldn't have gone from my forever
to my ex best friend

do you miss touching me?
i remember in the end there was barely any
touch at all
was my skin a poison?
everything about you was harder
harder to reach, harder to touch, harder to talk to
sometimes i wonder if all that was broken within
might've had a chance to heal
if you had opened yourself back up to me
if i had been given a chance to hold your heart again

it's a dangerous thing to live in i wonders

there were 748 things i want to say to you
i know because i tried to write them all down
at night they all rise up and wash over me
and i feel like i might drown
words words words
one of us grabbed hold of them like a lifeline
and the other chose to let them sink
it is a sad truth when you realize your person
no longer values the things you do
(no longer puts value in you)
so i crumple up all the long-held dreams
i once kept close to my heart
let their sad thoughts fade into oblivion

there were 748 things i wanted to say to you
but once this book is done, there will be none

Dabria Karapita-Parker

perhaps you will blame me for the bad times we had
perhaps you'll whisper in the next girl's head
that she's the fourth (fifth? sixth?) woman you've taken to bed
perhaps you'll tell her nothing at all
simply allow yourself to fall
perhaps this will simply become a faded bad dream
(so you'll tell yourself this time next year)

State of a Sunflower Soul

maybe you will tell people that you truly tried
who am i to invalidate what you'll call your experience?
(i stuff receipt upon receipt into a wooden drawer)
if you are going to insist on telling people
such a pretty, shallow lie
perhaps one day
you should try to include
the truth
of what happened
between you and i

healing only happens
when we allow ourselves to face the music
ugly as the tune may be

Dabria Karapita-Parker

Terror
notes on windshields
garage doors opening
startled faces
why do you have such a hard time letting me go?
you say you still dream of me
good, i hope i haunt you
and then one day
i hope
the ghost of me
leaves you too

State of a Sunflower Soul

i am a queen
with golden crown ablaze
they will throw slander
it will not touch me
they spew forth lies
yet still, i will rise
they think they broke me
but look in my eyes
i am a queen, warrior
i am soft heart, a soldier
i am unbroken, i smoulder

my fire will not dim

Dabria Karapita-Parker

you told me you'd regret all the places we never got to visit
well darling, i won't
you always pulled the joy from my wanderings
wrapped in a cold ease of logic
and i am so thrilled
that i am able to go back to exploring
my land, on my terms

i unpacked the boxes
your mother had stuffed in our garage
found the first married valentine card
we'd exchanged
i wonder if you cried as much as you said you did
in the 14-page sonnet which i never wanted
(i asked you for love letters
but only got a suicide note
from the marriage you killed)
you wrote such beautiful lies
if i didn't have space i would have almost believed them
while being a storyteller was always my heart
(re) writing the narrative was always
your favourite game to play

i'm done with games.

Gentle Love
i am overpowered
with loneliness
for another time
for dark star studded skies
a silver vehicle beaming in the moonlight
for whispered talks and quiet tears
and all the many ways we fell in love throughout the years
when i am lonely
i think about my best friend's heart around mine
and i dream about
another time

Numbers
i saw you on a dating app
and i almost couldn't breathe
my sister pointed out you used
one of our wedding photos
(looking dapper in a suit without me by your side)
it's been two months and ten days
since you put the fear of man into me
and that day
had been four and a half days after moving into our new house
and one year and twenty days after you had said i do

i saw you on a dating app today
(it's been two months and ten days
and i now choose to be unafraid)
i simply said a prayer for the girl who would be next

Dabria Karapita-Parker

Numbers + 1
it's been two months and eleven days
since i walked out the door of our house
with every intention to come back and stay

it's been two months and eleven days
since you drew the line in the sand
made it clear there would never be
any way back
from the person you had become
(you can only cross that line once
before i will never walk back in that door)

i've decided since then to stare into the face
of a raging beast to take back my power
count to ten
i'm the queen here again

you spin your own narrative
and tell your tall tales
but darling, i thought i always told you
honesty is the best policy?

there is a reason i always get
such good returns

Dabria Karapita-Parker

you drop bread crumbs
as if it will lead me
down the path of regret
as if you think i will miss you
as if my heart still holds sadness
as if you don't already know
that i am relishing this freedom
this unknown
this completion

you think
i give
a damn?
i have crawled on blistered elbows through the ashes
my fingernails caked with the dirt from my rebirth
i have drawn blood
from all the times i have
scratched the surface of possibility
weeped the ruins of my old life
and willed my bloody knees to stand
i have bathed in the fire of my growth
i have slumbered through the aching pains
you think you own my memory?
watch as it vanishes with the mist

remember that i rise like a Phoenix in my free birth

how is it that i do not think of you
except to be thankful you are not here at all?
galaxies are born and stars collide and i touch worlds
with the palm of my hand
you once said you glimpsed starlight in my eyes
no, you didn't

if you had, you would've seen
that mere man's hands
could not hold this profusion of light
exploding from within

Polaroid Memories

Dabria Karapita-Parker

it is not you that i miss
your presence, your touch, your smell
rather, the only thing i miss
is the familiarity and rhythm we had found in each other

i suppose i can miss what is no longer there

do i think of you?
perhaps not as often as i should
you have become a footnote to the story
a prologue i sometimes forget to read
yet, you were there
the words of us shaping who we would become
do i think of you enough?
i think of you just as much as i do
no more, no less
and that is enough

you used to ask me how i liked my eggs
you don't need to cater to me,
i replied
and yet, you did
this was how i thought you loved me
isn't it funny,
the little things in life we remember?

State of a Sunflower Soul

do you remember the mountains
the way the mist cleared up on that second day
the whole world felt washed in a sweet late summer rain?
i wish we could go back to that again
the way our eyes seemed opened
the way we sat on the side of the road
watching that baby mountain goat
the way you looked at me
like there was still beautiful possibility

i remember when you asked me
if you could hold my hand
the sweetest gesture in the world
i remember when i asked you what you were thinking
and you told me, "i want to kiss you"
i remember you asking me to marry you
i remember our adventures
i remember our dreams
i remember our late night fights
and hugs that seemed to heal our world

i remember all of it.

State of a Sunflower Soul

sometimes i look back on our memories
and i am still able to smile
at every long mile
we managed to conquer

Dabria Karapita-Parker

there are movies we will never watch
(together)
there are places we will never visit
(together)
there are tears we will never cry
(together)
there are days we won't think of the other
(ever)

and yet,
i still have so much love to give
to another

a friend's hand to hold
a family member's laugh tucked tight into my heart
a long plane ride to another land
a soft kiss placed on another's cheek

do you remember that time
we drove the icefields parkway
and we couldn't see the mountains
because the mist was so strong?
you were disappointed
and wanted to turn around
and simply go home
but we held on. we hoped.
and on that second day,
the sun shone so strong
that all those mists of doubt
were driven away
we made beautiful memories
our life could've been like that
if only you knew how to hold on

Nighttime
i hope i saturate you
i hope the essence of me
fills every gulp of air you breathe

Morning
i hope that you forget me
that i am an undetectable sense of loss
you can't quite put your finger on

it took you two months and fifteen days
to delete all the playlists i'd made
except for that one
you know the one i mean

does it remind you of our happier days?
our honeymoon season?
driving through mountains?
and conquering our family skeletons?
does it remind you that we once had dreams
that we could make our place in this world?

no matter how rocky our world seemed to get
just take me to the mountains, baby
the place where we could forget

to the man i loved, still do, still care
i'm not sure how I managed to hang on to you
with limp hands, perhaps
a willingness to let you go, should the need arise
and yet, and yet
here we are
all these years later
still resting in the warmth of the other person's eyes
it's nothing new
my best friend
this poem's for you
i love you

to my best friend:
my love for you is a hopeless thing
a bird with a shattered wing
we're going on six years strong
and there is a part of my heart
that doesn't want it to heal
that doesn't want to admit to myself
that i can do without you in my life
i want you, i want you
is my heart's whispered cry
i can't let you go
and i don't want to learn why

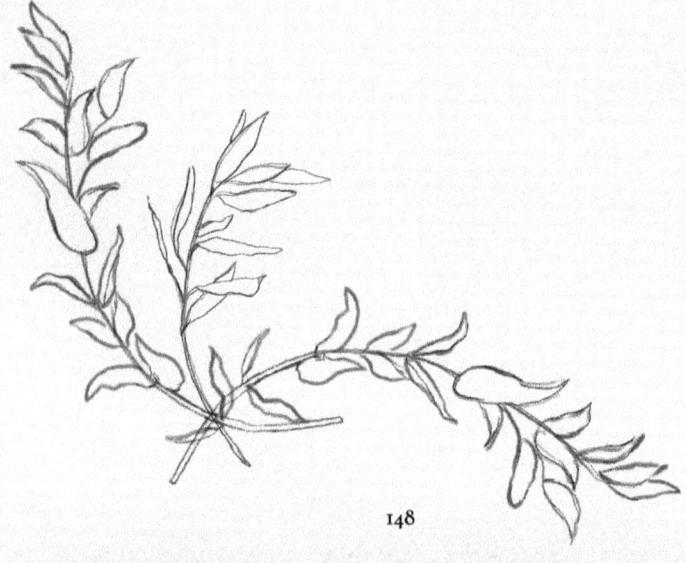

Dabria Karapita-Parker

i cried for my job, my car, my house
i cried when i said good bye to the ring
and when i walked out my house door for the final time
i cried for the dreams that got crushed
i cried for the realization
that when one person says "i do,"
sometimes it can still mean "they won't"

i cry. i release. i surrender all that i have given up
for the freedom of what will come next.

Vivian
deep red, velvet seats
a ride that could put a baby to sleep
my first car
my first kiss
our last drive
my head, on your lap
best friends
long drives
late nights
cruises through the mountainsides

you contain so many memories
i know it's gonna hurt when we say good-bye

Dabria Karapita-Parker

i had to make peace
with letting certain things go
otherwise i knew
those guillotined dreams
would eat me alive
and from the inside out

it is a relief to me
that there will be music
i listen to
that will not be saturated
with the presence of you
that there are places i will visit
that will not carry the weight
of a memory made with you

Re: Important
there might come a time
when you read this poetry book
and say to yourself
well, i gave her this
i hate to break it to you, my dear
but the only thing you gave to me
was the reminder of how much i am capable of
and that we always have the damn free choice
of what to do with the brokenness gifted to us by others
and the tendency towards self pity

(can't you tell? i suffocated it and wrote a book
with the ink from my soul)

State of a Sunflower Soul

i hope in some odd way
you relish your sad songs
play them on repeat
allow yourself to get lost
in their melancholic beat
then one day
i hope you wake up
decide you are fine
and move on with your life

don't make me into the unwilling paper weight
that holds the next chapter of your life down

Dabria Karapita-Parker

You're just somebody i used to know
campfire nights and just-like-a-sister fights
midnight McDonald's drive and moving in side by side
are we friends? will you be my sister?
i love your brother, i love i love i love
time passes. flowers grow. darkness covers. i curl into a tiny ball.
paste a smile and pretend we're alright. slowly die. glance at him
out of the corner of my eye.
how long can you hide?
that day you came to the mall with him
the terror in the faces of all who stood by my side.
i looked into your eyes
pleading, begging, gasping to my sister
i didn't ask for this fight
can't you see how scared i've been?
months pass and i come home.
one day i walk past your street, in the heart of my hometown
my heart sings its release
you're just somebody i used to know.

State of a Sunflower Soul

i am at peace
with polaroid moments
stuck on repeat
i am at peace
with releasing those dreams
i couldn't escape from even in sleep
i am at peace
with a moment of holding your hand
and the next, never again
i am at peace
knowing this season is done
and my heart has paved the way
for a new path to have begun

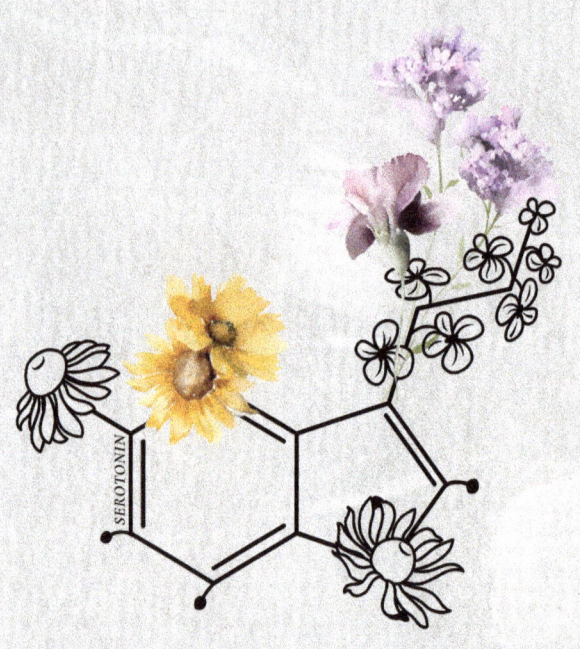

Sunlit Possibilities

Dabria Karapita-Parker

what do i feel
apart from the loss of you?

i blink my eyes in the bright sunlight of possibility

i'm learning about me again

State of a Sunflower Soul

it's been a long drought
i look up with a start
i'm out of your wasteland

i'm dancing again

Dabria Karapita-Parker

butterfly moments
i am learning to breathe in my own company again

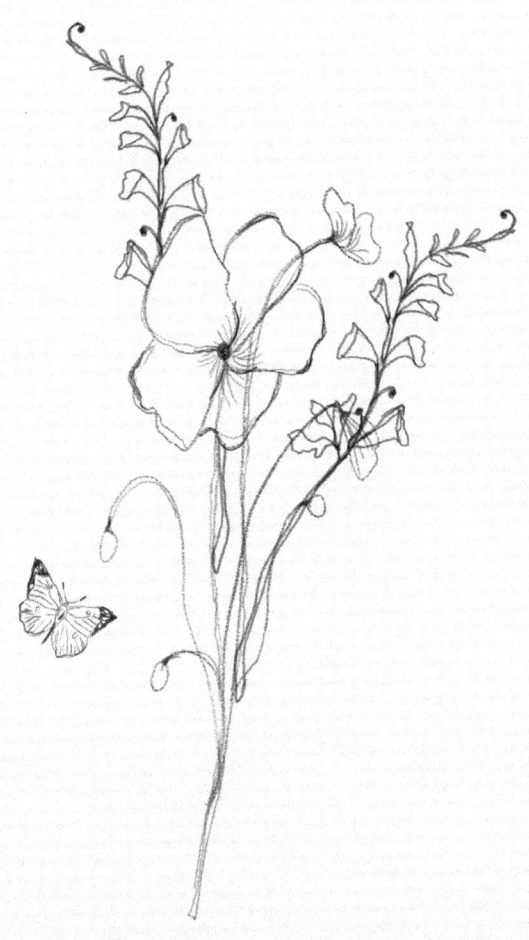

ink
the indelible art we make on our skin

art
the act of creating something from the passion in our blood

Dabria Karapita-Parker

who are you afraid of?
and why do you carry that
fear in your heart around
wherever you go?

-my heart now sings of its release

State of a Sunflower Soul

i reinvent for myself a second skin
a short time later i have to do it again
as of late i seem to shed more than a snake
one season i am cocooning
then opening up softly
i find myself malleable
then hard as granite
(the shattering had its purpose)
the sun goes down
and rises on yet another side of who i am

Dabria Karapita-Parker

what we give our focus to is what we become
this is a hard lesson, my lovelies
listen well
i decide to remember the beauty
so that i don't get stained by the years of ugly
this is always a choice

choose wisely

State of a Sunflower Soul

golden light hits the fields
and late afternoon sunlight
filters through the leaves
these are the things i'm noticing again
these are the things that tell me i feel alive again

Dabria Karapita-Parker

what a beautiful season for a breakup
the painted autumn leaves pool on the ground
like buckets of gold ripe for picking
they remind me of the joy of this season
the shedding of what's dead
to make room for new growth instead

you told me to be ashamed of my roots
to measure my success by how far
i could remove myself from them

when all hell broke loose
and i seemed on my own
it was those roots that wrapped themselves
around my heart

my defence in the madness
my stability in the uproar
my family

Dabria Karapita-Parker

red silk dress caresses my curves
dark brown hair kisses my neckline
i've learned to love this woman i've become
the person i've fought for
the battles i've won

State of a Sunflower Soul

what do i feel now?
freedom
the taste of it on my lips like
peaches

Dabria Karapita-Parker

i no longer toss and turn at night
with you in the bed beside me
wondering why it is you no longer hold me
i no longer cry myself to sleep
asking myself again and again why you have no desire for me
instead
as mad as it sounds
i close my eyes in this bed all alone
i sleep soundly

i've started dreaming again

State of a Sunflower Soul

there is breath in my lungs
a chill in the air
there are leaves slowly falling
and echoes of grace are everywhere

Dabria Karapita-Parker

i think we are going to be okay
this is my closure
i have prayed
and sobbed
and given the weight of it to God
wherever you are
i wish you no ill will
but i will no longer carry your unpaid bill
i let it go, i let the idea of us go

State of a Sunflower Soul

it rained last night
the grass smells like
the earth took a shower
the sunlight reflects
the water clinging to the orange leaves

it rained last night
my bed smells like
i've taken a shower
my new life reflects
i no longer cling to the sensation of you

i'm washed clean

Dabria Karapita-Parker

i no longer wear you as a loss
underneath my skin
i no longer hold all the words you said
as gold treasure kept shiny within

open palms
to the sky
i release all that is no longer mine
(have i been here before? this sacred act of letting go?)

you leaving
pushed me out of a
comfort zone
i didn't even know
i had come to live in

i don't think you understand
that i am perfectly happy without you
what room is there left in that?
except for me to say:

i've let you go
(i don't need to do it again)

i've said my goodbye
(and i won't let you back in)

State of a Sunflower Soul

there is freedom
and it feels like gratitude
riding on the winds of autumn

Dabria Karapita-Parker

i planted sunflowers in the garden of my heart
added the seeds of all the beauty in my life
tulips, roses, lilies, daisies
(gratitude, grace, choices, friendship)

i revelled in the freedom of my new garden

this is my one firm belief
that God's got this
this is the truth that i cling to
my God's got this
when anxiety threatens to overwhelm
God's got this
strength and courage sing like an anthem down my spine
God's got this

Sunflower

i think i am most happy
when i soak myself in words of grace
allow my attitude to be full
with gratitude
instead of hate
i choose to find growth
in the midst of this storm
turn my face to the sunlight
that always shines after rain

Thanksgiving
the sky is a muddied pink
like the curtains in the office we used to sleep
in and my mind drifts towards thoughts
of happiness and grace
it's thanksgiving twenty twenty one
and i have so much to be thankful for
thank you for the growing
the falling
the healing

on this note of gratitude
i am almost ready to close the chapter of this book
i am at peace with what did not work
courage lays its head at the base of my spine
and i let go of what's no longer mine

Dabria Karapita-Parker

10 • 14 • 21
the autumn leaves are falling
they paint the ground orange
marking the passing of time gone by
and the memories this season has made

i just came inside from burning our stuff
it amazes me how much of it you gave back
anniversary notes and little books and Christmas gifts
physical markers of the experiences we shared

there were some good times
as well as a lot of bad
the simple state of our life requires
carving a life out of the journey
never stop learning, never stop growing

when the cold gets here,
and i know it will
i remind myself i'm a sunflower
the way i've always found the light

when the next season comes
and the dreams i painted
on the canvas of my future come alive
i will not forget the starlight in my eyes
nor the mountains i have faced

in the starry evening light
i watched the flames travel to the sky
i close the chapter of you and i
i will not be weighed down
by the outline of our soul lines in the distance

remind me of this:
there is no regret

(Aftermath)

Aftermath

some chapters in life aren't all tied off pretty with a bow
we don't get closure in the form of a sincere apology
and there are days i still see reflections of you
in someone's black pea coat

regardless of the ending, it's a life lived in colours
since the day i walked away

this aftermath looks like a rainbow

the tiny tendrils that cling to you
like mud droplets splashing the bottom of my coat
the sad nighttime whispers
when you ask yourself if you'll ever truly be alright again
the way poems leak from you, ache in you,
crawl away from you
until it is dawn and the watery light sneaks in
and it is daylight again
and somehow you're okay again
(another night another poem)

healing is never linear

Prayer
i still pray for you
pray that you will never confess to another girl you love her
then set the safe place she's curated with you on fire
i pray that you will begin to bleed like a normal man again
pray that you will learn to apologize like a human again
i pray that you will one day look yourself in the mirror
eye to eye and your soul stripped before the gaze of God
and on bended knee you will become
the man i once vowed to love
the man who at one time held my heart, my life, my hand

i pray i will not be there to see this sign of new life
grace your cheeks again
but i do pray one day we will be able to live
whole, separate, at peace with God and forgiven

Ghosting
haunted steps and haunting breaths
breathe in breathe out
you're okay
you no longer hold the haunting of me in your hands
you no longer hold any of me at all
except a small piece of history in my heart
a fissure healed
a crack sealed

Poet

my heart bled ink
wax melted on the skin of my hands
i wrote and i wrote
until my heart had been fed
and my mind relieved
until i no longer bled poetry
that reeked of you
my story is my own now

you are but a footnote.

New Year's Resolution
shrugging off insecurity
like the heaviness of a soaked towel
let it fall to the floor
walk forward, unhindered

this is me shedding the weight of the past

Dabria Karapita-Parker

i've always been a sunset girl
even things that fall will rise again soon

Melody
i have loved
i have lost
and i have gained
an anthem of grace
that sings in the movement of these bones
that sings as the song of my soul

Dabria Karapita-Parker

Rise
take courage, heavy heart
whisper it to yourself
even in the dark days of winter
dawn still rises

Losing

i miss the friend you were to me
late night talks in an abandoned church parking lot
the prayer on my lips that you would see me
the same way i looked at you
in a kaleidoscope of memories and emotions
with a smile that said, *i see you, i want you*
the chill in the front seat as our eyes met
and the warmth in our breaths as our souls leapt
brave in the understood meaning
we held between us like a shared secret
brave as my heart, splayed out on the black leather seat

Whiskey Shots

it's 10pm on a Friday night
i've drunk three shots of whiskey and
it's your name that is on my lips
i don't drink much anymore
not since the fall of the wall of babel
(the ex that brought nothing but confusion in his wake)
but every once in a while on a Friday night
i sip my forty percent and imagine what it would be like
to have your arms come around me and to feel wanted
by the person i used to love
i suppose that's the whiskey talking

but i wish it was my lost best friend

Fading
sometimes the loss creeps up on you
in the aisles of the grocery store

we can't live in the past
feeding off the vibrancy of old memories
we have to walk forward
creating our own new ones

i reach for a carton of milk and i am aware
that one day i will not see
your face reflected in the glass

Dabria Karapita-Parker

we imagine the other as stagnant
permanently frozen in the lives we knew them to lead
i hope this isn't true
i hope you decide to replace your car
i hope you find a new recipe to create
i hope you dye your hair
change your style
go someplace you haven't been in awhile
i hope the essence of me covers you
but only for a season
i hope you grieve me (fiercely)
i hope you miss me (softly)
i hope the memories of me put a smile on your face
then, one morning
i hope the sun rises
finding you in a new place

{ back when we were lovers }
alternating rings on my left hand
we stained this city with our moments
burning our love as a never failing indentation into
the streets we came to call home
the city lights towered and glowed
in the windshield behind us
i looked at you
wondering if forever had found us
the rearview mirror began to narrow
you looked at me
you looked
you

Soft Yellow

like the lamp in my living room
casting shadows across the wall
golden yellow like the glass of liquor in my hand
bright yellow like the sunlit days we used to explore
intertwined, fate yet undetermined
soft like the peace i now find in sleep

White
it is only in the late nights of this white winter
that your name makes me pause
the *could've beens* creep up on me like the chill
of a late fall day when i forgot
to bring my white sweater along
and i am besotted
with wiping every last trace of you from my lips
my phone my eyes my teeth my life
i am obsessed
with making sure you are never my obsession again
you made your bed
now you lie in it alone
in another house i pull satin sheets up to my chin
finally allowed to breathe again

Slate Grey
the colour of sidewalks after rain and the essence
in the air after i've whispered your name
grey like the fibres of my living room carpet, like the ground
outside the movie theatre we used to go to
the old ticket in my pocket is crumpled
like the debts from our past
like your grey sock i found in the drawer today
day melts into night and i am left to explore
the city lights echoing against
the silhouettes of darkened skyscrapers
rushing reminders of the friendship you used to be
i am staring into the night sky,
tendrils of vapour rising from my chest
brushing tenderness away from the webs of my heart
like a slate grey chalkboard being wiped clean

Blue
there were blue Christmas lights
hanging off the edges of the roof.
brighter blue than the colour of your eyes
that same afternoon you threw the towel in.
threw the rage you'd kept bottled up into my face,
locked the door and threw away the key.
my sweater was a lighter blue the winter day
i walked up the porch steps.
light blue like the colour of the ocean canvas
that hangs in my new living room.
the look in your face as the door swung open to greet me,
like the house knew i was its owner, knew i would be back,
knew i would be fearless.
the drop in my stomach.
the steel in my spine.
i handed you the Christmas bow-wrapped gift
i'd had sitting in my own porch for the past month.
your shock registered, my smile grew.
they say don't fight fire with fire so i reached inside my heart for a bucket of calmed water.
the lights reflected blue on my coat shoulders
as we leaned in for a hug.
you said, "i miss you," in the curve of your spine.
i said, "i'd miss me too," in my silent reply.
you wanted to invite me in but little you knew,
i had gotten up off of bruised knees
from our constant fights and I flew.
and after this day i would never, ever, ever come back to you.

Dabria Karapita-Parker

Rust Red

i was cleaning my house and i came across a black box
that held the golden necklace we'd bought
on our honeymoon trip to the coast
i pulled it out and looked close
its gold colour was hidden by a profusion of colours
that had exploded
all over its rose stem of a design
i scratched at its surface with my thumb nail
stared in awe at the rainbow petals,
deep red and dark blue, and wondered
how something so beautiful had changed its form
rusted
yet became more beautiful still

Evergreen
the day draws to a close
i peel my work clothes off
slip an evergreen sweatshirt
straight from the thrift store on.
my mother always told me
to wash the things i bring home first
mother, i've done a reckless thing
brought you into the home of my soul.
so i leave the bag of your old clothes
on the floor of my porch closet
dance around my living room
in my underwear and sweatshirt
i peel back the covers of my duvet and watch
as my dog finds a nook in which to lay.
the next day dawns dark in the winter's light
water, lemon, dash of caffeine
pull the mascara wand through the black tangle of my lashes.
kiss my dog's head, open the closet, lock the front door
i walk down the hallway black bag in hand
open the garbage chute drop it in walk away
i don't once turn around and look back
the evergreen sweatshirt caresses my neckline

finally, something reckless that's mine.

Pink

there is this reckoning
which rises to the surface
when you finally find the courage to utter the words,
yes, it was abuse.
and it is
pink
like the inside of my cheek from all the times
i felt the need to bite my tongue
the pink of grief of loss of world undone
pink
like the shirt of the man who asked me out on Valentine's Day
(one week exact from the signing of my freedom papers)
pink like the curtains that hang in my glorious bedroom
pink like my dog's harness which i allow to come undone
pink like the sunrise of a stunning May day
like the blossoms in my living room
like my favourite colour
of strength of resilience of endurance

State of a Sunflower Soul

thirteen days after i signed my divorce papers
i took a solo trip
drove 9+ hours in my vehicle
with my blasting thoughts and quiet music
i went to a huge mall all by myself and
bought myself every good thing
he would've given me trouble for
i paid for my own damn things!
i got a golden nose ring!
i painted my nails blood red!
i bought myself jewelry like there was no tomorrow!
i ate ice cream and creamy pasta and
chugged costly fuji water!
i walked around and revelled in the fact that
i am my own woman and
i am fierce and i am strong
soft heart, releasing my fears in trails down my cheeks
wise soul, picking my knees up off the floor
and crossing through doors

i am wild i am free i am...

home, part 1

my heart has held many homes this past year
and i have been thankful for this glimpse
of a future i got to hold
i have been thankful for the memories, the family, the hope
i have grappled through the grieving, the fear, the loss
despite the night there is always hope
the moon rises and ocean waves crash and
there is always a fresh sunrise to breathe in
(the future always looks bright again)

this is the cycle of life and death, begin

home, part 2
i've said goodbye to three of my houses in less than a year
(four if you count the rooms i thought i held in your soul)
the first was the transitional place
the place above ground that housed our first married love
strewn were the memories of our early times all across its floors
second, a house with lots of free space supposed to be
our foundational, yet ended up being the confessional
where all the secrets got found and the locks got changed
and i walked up its steps on a blue winter's day to hand you
a Christmas present and take back my closure
now this final place, to which i will soon say goodbye,
was a safe haven for this gypsy soul just landed
fairy lights and late friendship nights
i moved the recliner to the centre of the room
for a better view of the sunset
just because i could, just because i'm free
its walls have held the healing,
the nights of constant tearing, my prayers,
my release
it has been a *gift*
but i hold these hands out with the knowledge
that when we let things go
bigger things have room to flow
i always knew i had a gypsy soul
and while i stand in awe
grateful for the houses that have held me
in the midst of all my moving

i now know that i am my truest home.

Summer/Autumn

isn't it strange to think
there will be someone after you?
that there will be someone after him
before i finally feel at peace again
for so long i felt stained
coloured by the essence of you

isn't it interesting to think
that someone else will stain me too?

State of a Sunflower Soul

it was a beach
six of us apiece
and you sneaking a look at me

it was a heat wave
your beach mat next to mine
and my way of seeing us intertwined

a few weeks later
there was a backyard shaped as our own personal graveyard
a starlit night, the perfect fright
an apple tree hung above us
our lips met, the summer truly began

Dabria Karapita-Parker

whiplash
road rash
keep your heart firmly attached
new move
sudden midnight proof
that you'll be alright
we had so many beautiful summer moments
they don't have to be coated in the taste of sadness
a car drives down a highway
speeds up under the canopy of starlight
my chest matches its thunderous heartbeat

State of a Sunflower Soul

i suppose all good things must come to an end
like seeing your hoodie pop out your front door on a hot
summer evening and first time drives
through darkened neighbourhoods
metal music blasting through the streets
like watching arms spread candy yellow wax
on a car and wondering
to myself how far how far how far
will you take us
how far will you let us go
the fragrant smell of candle
a ruined keyboard and marble blue romper
weighted blankets
the weight of you
these things will always remind me
of a summer spent with you
these memories i'll take with me when i go

Dabria Karapita-Parker

it is summer nights
fully embracing life
and being sad sometimes
it's liking an emo boy
with hair blonde as white silk
who carries a taste in music that stretches the limit
inked hands trail up thighs
late nights opening up deep insights
why is fear still trying to live in the cracks between these bones?
is the question my heart sometimes
whispers, standing in the balcony sun
i watch as the autumn sky prepares to bring slow changes
rebirth
dawn

there was a time
when i was an excited university student
and the colour of autumn leaves littered the path
to an unknown future
there was a time
when i was a summer's blushing bride
and the white silk of a ballgown got tangled up with the
grey cloud of an unimaginable future
there was a time
when we sat together in a car in the moonlight
when our heartstrings were intertwined
when the hands on the clock dial inched forward
when we sped down the highway beneath a sheet of stars
when i walked myself home after a warm night of dancing
when i started watching the sunsets again
when i cried on my kitchen floor
when i released what was no more
who knows how we will end up being defined?
the only story i can tell is my own
the future lies there, unwritten
there was a time
there was time
there, time
time

Phantom

i don't like things left unfinished
but this phantom called Closure,
well it haunts me
the essence of relationships undone
the spool of connection dropped and abruptly untouched
the way we looked at each other like it was
just another time
not *the* last time
the way i closed the door on a blue house
the way i packed up a grey box and put it in the closet
do you ever think of all the ways you still play into another's story?
i don't like things left messy, unfinished
and yet this is what my life has tossed to me
Phantom runs a weary hand over his eyes
his chest is empty, and my heart is full
of all the ways i've come undone
and wrapped myself back together again

there are so many people i want to text
do you regret
that we met?
is what i often find bubbling on the edge of my tongue
do you wish
we'd never met?
what i really want to ask is:
if you could go back would you do it again?
would you still reach out with open arms,
say those words, risk the time,
rest your naked forehead against mine?

am i still worth it, despite the end?

driving away from what had been my home
three times over we play this tune
(april fools turned into september blooms)
arriving at my family's farm
the night enfolded me
the autumn leaves lay quieted in the dark
the stars rang clear and untangled
in the liquid navy sky through my sunroof
as i watched the road unfold before me
in the pools of my headlights
all that had been merged into the lane of *all that can be*
joy teased my fingertips as hope sprang alive
for the first time in a long time i felt like
i am finally okay
i am breathing deeply again
and like a deer caught in a net of sudden light

i realize i no longer feel the brokenness
in my ribs between breath

State of a Sunflower Soul

i moved back to my hometown for a season
and it was spring, and the roads were slick
with the promise of all that could come

summer slowed its roll
cabarets ran full toll
beach days and camping days and
do nothing days became the norm

slowly autumn creeped on
i went away to the mountains
grief lingering on the edge of my vision
as i drove away from my hometown

now it's fully autumn, and the life i've lived
lays curled up in the yellow-tinged leaves
of the trees i so often walked past
soon i will pack my life away and move
on the path of a new adventure

nostalgia has always been my most loyal companion
just this time, i wish it would leave itself behind
and allow me this gentle freeing

Dabria Karapita-Parker

you remember the times when you were little
and moving meant boxes and boxes of excitement
it meant a new place and wrapped plates
and takeout for a week straight
it meant sleeping on your mattress on the floor
people come to help walking through your front door
then you grow up…
moving is now juggling full time work
and packing late into the night and a few sighs
it means wrestling with the thoughts
of what you're leaving behind
it is not always closure

who's to say we don't make our own?
the future awaits
a kaleidoscope of unmarked paper
it means a different kind of adventure
one you alone get to write

i take a break and roll the pictures
from my walls in blankets and
drink warm coffee in the sunlight
is this what being grown up looks like?

i sat down and tried to write a happy poem
because there is still good that permeates this living
i sat down and tried to write a happy poem
and i put away thoughts of packing up
sad goodbyes in pretty boxes
i sat down and tried to write a happy poem
i thought of warm summer nights
the smell in the air at dawn and
my hand lingering in your palm
i sat down and tried to write a happy poem
the way the beach caressed my tired soul touched my heart
awakened my dreams again
the darkened pavement flying beneath bicycle wheels
with friends at midnight
ice cream that melted on fingers and coffee together
walking through my old neighbourhood
i sat down to write a happy poem

then realized I was the happy one instead

the words "*i am thankful*" do not seem to take up enough space
for what it is i really want to say

(i am thankful i survived a devastating season of life
thankful for the moments of grace that lent beauty to my life
i am thankful for the friends who showed up
again and again and again and again
and yet
i can still find gratitude for the people who walked away
and allowed me to turn the page
i can't find enough words to show my gratitude and love
for my family who became a well of hope
i could draw from in my darkest night
i am thankful for the circumstances
that whittled away dead branches
and gave new life to these roots
i am thankful for this season of hope)

the sun shines golden today
and there is so much joy coating the air
thanksgiving twenty twenty two
i am thankful for you

State of a Sunflower Soul

i used to be terrified of driving around curves too fast
i never used to enjoy hiking down steep nature paths
or walking through these neighbourhoods
again and again
soft serve ice cream was my least favourite
i'd always skip through metal music
time rolls by and the cities i've lived in change
i have been house to house and heart to heart
for a very long while
suddenly i'm uncovering layers to this heart
i never knew could exist
i'm discovering that i can find new favourite things
and nothing is set in stone
turn the music dial up
the smell of warm apple wafts through this place

i'm so deliciously happy
that is something else i never thought i'd learn

Dabria Karapita-Parker

Honey

my mom asked me to write a happy poem
after so long of sifting through
the bleak fog of grief and sadness
how do i tell her i'm doing okay again?
that things are looking up the way the sunrise
ignites the corner of my apartment
the way i wrap myself in blankets and trace steps
from big dipper to ursa major
there was a time when i couldn't
see my way out of the darkness
when anxiety laid its head like a weight on my chest
those days are fewer now, mom
i'm throwing open my balcony door
i'm letting the wildness in
i'm calling my friends
i'm eating the meals
and i've found the strength to pick up my pen
how do i tell you i'm happy now, mom?
i'm drinking honey in my coffee again

State of a Sunflower Soul

i have friends who have been there
for me in ways i've not deserved
held my hand as i walked through destruction
i have people in my life who have walked in then out
at just the right moments
blessing, lesson, lesson
prayers that were answered in ways
i could never have imagined
pain i walked through that at times
felt like i wouldn't survive
i used to hold on to my dead ends with such fondness
and yet
forgiveness, redemption, great grace
in this new season pours down
such hope coming alive in these limbs again
after so long of feeling coloured
by the lingering essence of pain
please, allow me to admire the way
the light comes in the windows
it has been too long since i have stayed
in one place and made a home
i finally feel like me again

Dabria Karapita-Parker

i woke up
and it was soft like Sunday morning
and my limbs ached
it was an odd in between
a crossfading connecting
all that has passed and all this is about to be

there was longing beneath these teeth again
to taste of potential to come
a life packed up in boxes
can mean moments drawing to a close
but stepping forward leaves room
for emptied shelves to be filled again

(*can we begin life again, again?*)
(*and so i begin again, again*)

State of a Sunflower Soul

like the seed
that has to die
for roots to begin
i will rise
and like the sunflower
that always turns
its head towards the sun
even in the darkest night
i will look for the light
whatever it takes
it's the perpetual state
of a sunflower soul
that i will choose to live in
over and over again

Letter to my women,

i know the world is swirling right now. questions abound and there don't seem to be any answers found. night falls and the silence creeps in and the doubts arise. *did he ever truly love me at all? why did he change so completely, so instant? was it real? why wasn't i enough?*

beautiful woman, with your eyes hewn from hope, and a heart that's alight (with beauty and fondness, strength and sacrifice) it was not you that was lacking.

it was never you that wasn't enough.

from the beginning you believed the best in that someone— you carried that hope, that trust, that love, and slowly in this life you began to level up.
time passed and that person's smallness (in life, in mindset, in lack of growth) began to show.
sometimes they attempt
to put that smallness on you.
don't let them.

i have seen that despite the heartbreak, you show up. while questions remain, you continue to love. don't ever question whether you were worth their time. their inability to level up with you, work with you, reconcile the truth
(in authenticity, honesty, love)
is a reflection of their life's path,
not yours.

remind your soul of its deepest worth.
remind your heart of the unchanging, unfailing love of God (call a friend, write a poem, put on a song, cry a lot)

grief is not linear, but you are so strong.

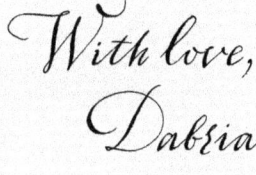

Prologue

The Edge of Ivy

24 Going On 25

i'm getting married in fourteen sleeps
that's not something i thought i'd say again for a long while
and this whole process of growing up has
been like cutting teeth
like making my insides bleed
like trimming the ivy of growth
tangled up inside of me
from being twenty four going on twenty five
feeling like thirty seven trips around the sun

has it only been my heart that has been
scorched and drowned and born afresh
again in a brilliant emerald green?
has it been only me to taste it all and feel
nothing a little, and lay my head down for another renewal?
only to be reminded again that i'm only
twenty four going on twenty five
the teeth will cut and the heart will burn
and the growth will peek its head out again
to find the sun

all of this life lived has only been a prologue
of all that is still to come
i walk the line of growth
bathing at the edge of ivy

About the Author

At six years old, Dabria Karapita-Parker cracked open a notebook and attempted to write her first novel. Then, she started a newspaper for her Sunday school class at the age of eight. From that point on, she has journaled and recorded her life, feelings, and experiences through the eyes of ink.

Over the years, her ardent love of words has combined with her deepest passion: to help women find their voice.

After going through a shattering divorce at the age of twenty-two, Dabria once again put pen to paper and began the cathartic release of healing through poetry—writing about the pains of growing up, the slow unfolding/healing from abusive experiences, and discovering beauty in the aftermath.

State of a Sunflower Soul is her first published book of poetry, a book curated to flow with the ups and downs of the healing process.

Through her brand, DKP Creatives, Dabria hosts her podcast "Your Double Dose of Dabria," works as a professional emcee, and is writing her next book. She also currently works for a national network of radio stations in Canada. A proud Saskatchewan girl, she can often be found soaking in the prairie sunshine with her rescue dog Mango, going on adventures with her husband Benjamin, or crafting her next book idea (or two or three!).

To follow along with her on the journey,
go to: dkpcreatives.com

www.ingramcontent.com/pod-product-compliance
Lightning Source LLC
Chambersburg PA
CBHW040639100526
44585CB00039B/2876